D1738614

BUSH TUCKER MAGIC

EDITED BY
Jan Palethorpe

FREMANTLE ARTS CENTRE PRESS

First published 1997 by
FREMANTLE ARTS CENTRE PRESS
193 South Terrace (PO Box 320), South Fremantle
Western Australia 6162.

Ngunga Designs, 15 Stanley Street (PO Box 642), Derby, WA, 6728
Telephone 0819 911128, Facsimile 0891 911158.

Designed by John Douglass.

Typeset by Fremantle Arts Centre Press
and printed by South China Printing Co. Ltd., Hong Kong.

National Library of Australia
Cataloguing-in-publication data

Bush tucker magic

ISBN 1 86368 186 8.

1. Cookery, Australia. 2. Food in art – Australia.
I. Palethorpe, Jan, 1956– .

artswa
The State of Western Australia has made an investment in this project
through the Department for the Arts.

Cover: Jeanette Ishigushi, *Roggii's Walkabout*, 1996, silkscreen on fabric.
Endpaper: April Wilson, *Meeting Place*, 1996, silkscreen on fabric.

INTRODUCTION

I lived in the Kimberley for only three years. It's a beautiful, rugged and timeless place, full of food and stories ... if you can find them. Every Aboriginal person I met loved bush tucker, and most loved the opportunity to get out in the bush and go hunting and fishing. I've been lucky enough to experience some unforgettable bush trips; always with loads of kids piled high into the back of someone's Toyota, along with dogs, fishing nets, maybe a gun, tea bags, flour, sugar and the inevitable Sunshine powdered milk tin — the essential multi-purpose culinary utensil of the Kimberley. This book was inspired by such bush experiences and working alongside Aboriginal artists.

I first tasted sugarbag (bush honey) when Becky, her sister and the kids from Doon Doon Station took me out to their country, past Turkey

Creek in the North-East Kimberley. We all piled into the back of the Toyota with an old axe and one empty Sunshine tin, and drove through parched, amethyst-studded riverbeds to where the white-trunked bush honey trees grow.

The people spotted some trees which had that 'black pointy thing pointing out' and we all took turns at hacking into the trunk with a very blunt axe which kept flying off its handle. The little 'sugar flies' (native bees) buzzed as we pulled out sticky, lovely honey and bright cadmium-yellow eggs from deep inside the tree. We ate the honey there and then and it was wonderful, superb, unlike anything I've ever tasted. It's hard to explain the complexity of bush honey; like tasting eternity — so profound it could never be manufactured.

Our neighbours in Derby, who came from Wangkatjungka, returned from Fitzroy Crossing one day with a prize they'd caught on the way — a huge goanna. They borrowed our axe to make a fire in the backyard, promising us some when it was done. A modern gas stove just doesn't compare with the ground oven, and it will always be the only way to cook bush tucker. The reptile tasted rather like smoky chicken that night, but the charred black foot, complete with claws, looked pretty unappetising the next day sitting cold in our fridge.

Another time when I was making prints with artists in Oombulgurri (near Kalumburu and Wyndham), Mary took us fishing in her country, of which she is the traditional custodian. The people hooked an old rickety trailer onto the back of a small tractor and piled it up with kids, dogs and all the gear — it was a very uncomfortable ride but worth it. We drove to the river through miles of the most spectacular country I've ever seen. As soon as the fish were caught in the net, they were cooked whole on the coals — not scaled, gutted and beheaded, and no salt, herbs or sauces. We washed them down with hot billy tea boiled in the Sunshine tin. Mary made some damper and cooked it in the coals. While the children played in the river she broke off small pieces and put them in the branches of the tree above her head, keeping them safe and clean for the kids.

Once I went out fishing with Ngunga Women's Group to May River near Windjana Gorge. On arrival one of the old ladies plunged her arm up to the elbow in sand, and pulled out little burrowing sand frogs. They were hooked onto the fishing line for barramundi bait.

The contributors in this book are all a part of Ngunga Designs in Derby, a screen-printing studio and shop conceived and operated by Aboriginal women as 'women coming together and talking'. All titles appear as spoken, some are in the Nyigina lanuguage, others are spelt phonetically or in English.

This collection of prints and recipes was gathered over cups of tea at Ngunga Designs. Everyone there had recipes to contribute. Most of the screen-prints were originally designed for application to fabric, and all the linoprints were designed to illustrate this book.

I have participated in many projects with Ngunga Designs and it has been a joy to work with such talented and energetic women.

The artists from Ngunga Designs all live in and around Derby, in the remote North-West Kimberley. They probably don't get out on long bush trips as much as they would like, but they often go down to the jetty and try their luck catching mud crabs, stingrays, barramundi and catfish. And as Kathy says, 'when we got no tucker, we got bush tucker.'

Jan Palethorpe

Jalgamugudah
(MUDSHELLS)

Some shells we eat too in the mangrove. Just throw 'em on the coals — all the meat come out, sometime you gotta hit it.

Hit it with a rock. When it's raw, it's good for colds. It's green and slimy. It's got a shell like a cone. It camouflages with the mud.

Valerie Lennard

Cecelia Riley, *Mudshells*, 1996,
silkscreen on fabric.

Bush Pudding

When you grab 'em boab nuts, smash 'em, skin 'em and take those nuts out. And you go home, and you get a billycan and fill 'em up with water and put 'em boab fruit. Put 'em inside the water now. You get the sugar (up to you how much you want to put 'em). Mix 'em up now, after a while it get yellow, then, I'll tell you you'll never stop eating that.

If we got no tucker, we got bush tucker. Just like a custard.

Kathy Bird

JUANDA
(BUSH ONION)

You dig 'em from the ground, they're very small and round — dark brown skin. You can eat 'em raw or throw it on the coals.

Annette Riley

Annette Riley, *Juanda* (Bush Onion), 1996, linoprint on paper.

SWORDFISH

You guts it out, then you just fry it with its own fat. Some people eat the fat from the stomach raw. Fry it the same as all fishes. You can cook shark the same way.

Valerie Lennard

Jeanette Ishigushi, *Shark's Journey*, 1996, silkscreen on fabric.

© NG IN IA DESIGNS DERBY WA JEANETTE HUNTER

GINNUP
(STINGRAY)

You put it on the coal, and the fat you just put in a pot and mix it with the meat. It's lovely, the three of them, they're all nice (stingray, shark and swordfish).

Valerie Lennard

Antoinette Hunter, *Stingray*, 1996, silkscreen on fabric.

Bush Honey

Just say you're going hunting or fishing near the river. Take your axe and, well if you see the little flies ... (you can see all the little honey flies going around the tree). You walk to the tree, you see a little pointy wax poking out — black or brown — it's hard to see. Some people can hear the bees. Then you go from underneath, sometimes you go from the sides or underneath it, that's where you chop it, chop away 'til you find the honey and the eggs ... yellow eggs.

Fill it up in your billycan or cup. You can eat it straight from the tree like that. They call it sugarbag.

Cecelia Riley

Annette Riley, *Bush Honey Flies*, 1996, linoprint on paper.

BUSH ORANGE

They're green and dark green too, the skin when they ripen they're pink inside, the fruit what you eat. Some, people, if it's still hard they bury 'em in the sand for two days. It gets soft and they eat it then. Some are sweet and some are bitter.

It looks more like a bush guava or a lemon.

Annette Riley

MANBUG
(SAND FROG)

You get a stick. You track 'em where you walk when you go fishing in river. You find 'em that place now. Well, they're all over the soft sand now. Find 'em that place ... spot where they make his home ... look like a hump. Dig it with your hand, stick first, then when you find that frog, pull 'em outside now.

Long as you got your fire, when the coals are ready put 'em in the coals. Then cover him over with the coals. Taste like chicken.

You just eat the body and the flesh and throw the head away.

Kathy Bird

Linda De Lower, *Frog*, 1996, linoprint on paper.

Magabala
(BUSH BANANAS)

When they grow and they fruit, they never grow in the same spot, they move to another spot. They're long like a tear drop. The big ones you can peel it and eat the inside ... the flesh is white.

Some people chuck 'em in the ashes.

Annette Riley

Valerie Lennard, *Bush Fruits*, 1996, linoprint on paper.

NYIMMUNBURR
(FLYING FOX)

It's got a horrible smell in it — after it's cooked it's all right. You stone it with a shanghai or you can catch 'em in the caves (Windjana).

Then you got to light fire again, the same way. You burn the feathers — tip 'em over then you wait 'til the coals get hot 'til the fire dies down. Maybe you can just put 'em in Alfoil or just chuck 'em in like that. Tastes like chicken.

Pamela Marshall
and Valerie Lennard

Pamela Marshall, *Flying Fox*, 1996,
linoprint on paper.

CROC

Same ... cook all your bush things in a hole in the ashes.

They take out all the stomach and intestines — put it in the coals. It curls up and when it's cooked you just pull it out and eat it.

The smell is strong ... it stays in your body.

Kathy Bird

Nicki Dawson, *Croc*, 1996, linoprint on paper.

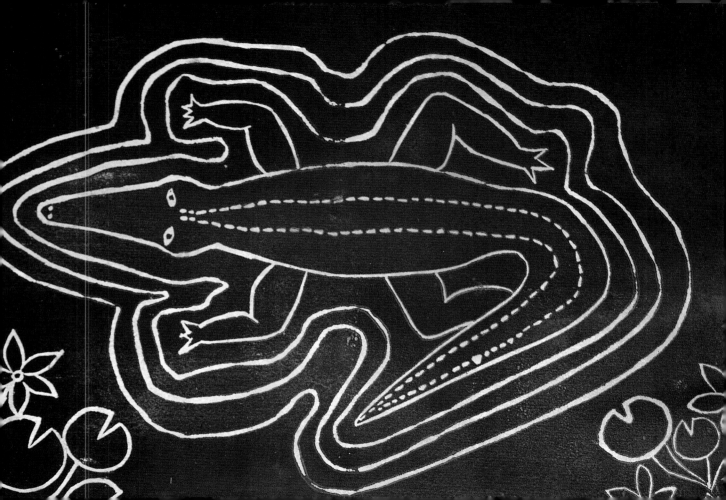

Nyilli Nyilli
(BUSH BUBBLEGUM)

They grow on vines in the tree in the bush. It's a sort of reddy–whitey colour. They're like pear shapes, and they hang up on the tree. They hang in bunches like bananas. Don't eat 'em when it's green, they burn your tongue. They're like orchids, it's like another tree attached to the tree.

When you grab the Nyilli Nyilli, you sqeeze 'em in a bunch in your mouth. They get all sticky like chewing gum. You can chew it and swallow it. We eat palm tree seeds as well — the dates.

Cecelia Riley

Pamela Marshall, *Patterns*, 1996,
linoprint on paper.

Witchetty Grubs

Just dig up around the trees, if you see where they left the mark from the roots under the ground. Like a big caterpillar, it comes out of the ground, especially after the rain. You get a crowbar or a big stick and start digging the roots.

They're shiny ... you can get about three or four. You have to break the roots to get 'em out.

Then you make a fire, throw 'em in the ashes on top 'til they get brown. Cool 'em off and you can eat 'em. Just like chicken. Lovely.

Linda De Lower

Linda De Lower, *Witchetty Grubs*, 1996, linoprint on paper.

GUNGGARA
(KOOGA BERRIES)

You just find 'em in the rainy season, on the prickly, bushy trees. They got skinny light green leaves and when they're raw, they're green — and when they're ripe they go black and they go a real purply shiny black. You just grab 'em off the tree and eat 'em. They're good for you. The tree itself is good for keeping away mosquitoes.

The dry wood from underneath, you smoke 'em babies. Dig a hole, make a fire then throw some green grass on top. Sprinkle water on top (keeps the evil away) then you just run the baby through the smoke. It makes the babies strong, so they don't have sickness. If people die, we cut that kooga berry and smoke 'em inside first and outside, to keep the spirits away.

Annette Riley

Cecelia Riley, *Kooga Berries*, 1996,
linoprint on paper.

OCTOPUS

Well you can lift the rocks, and find the octopus. You grab it with your hands, as long as it's not the wrong one (the poisonous one, Blue-ring), throw it on the rock.

We got all ways of cooking it. You can fry it, you can soak it in soya sauce or any sauce and steam it. People cook their octopus in different ways ... Chinese ... Japanese. I know some people who cook their octopus in hot tea. You know that skin ...? To peel it off. You boil it in tea to get the skin off. I never tried it. I was just told it!

Cecelia Riley, Valerie Lennard
and Annette Riley

Jeanette Ishigushi, *Sea Life*, 1996,
silkscreen on fabric.

WILD CAT

Catch it the same way like a kangaroo. Hit 'em across the neck, take 'em
back to dinner camp ... the bush, and make a big fire. After that fire make
a big hole, put that fire in the hole and wait 'til he get hot inside. Then put
the wild cat in ... you don't take the skin off. Just eat the body (not this
one, the head). Like a rib bone inside, like fresh meat. That's it.

Kathy Bird

NGULYUK
(BLUE TONGUED LIZARD)

They call 'em blue tongue. Well you grab 'em and find a stick and hit 'em across the head. You pick it up and make a fire.

You gotta wait for the coals in the fire and just put 'em on top that's all. Wait 'til they get cooked. Take the skin out and they got the meat inside, they got rib bones. Eat it up.

All my kids eat that — bush tucker — they learn it from their grandfather.

Kathy Bird

Halimah Bin Karim, *Mating Ngulyuk*, 1996,
silkscreen on fabric.

NGUNGA DESIGN © ARTIST HALIMAH · BIN · KARIM ·95·

BUNINGBURR
(BLACK-HEADED PYTHON)

The quiet one. You hit it with a stick across the neck then you cook 'em in
a hole in the ground oven. Tie up the snake with wire first. Tastes like ...
good ... like meat.

Agnes Bird

Josie Drummond, *Buningburr*, 1996,
silkscreen on fabric.

Barni
(GOANNA)

Sometimes with a spear you kill 'em. You gotta track 'em first, like emu tracks. You chase 'em with a stick or stone ... anything. Hit 'em across the head, make a fire first and make a hole then put stones inside the fire.

Put 'em in now. We don't eat that head, we chuck 'em out. We eat tail and some arms and the guts (liver).

Kathy Bird

Agnes Bird, *Bush Goanna*, 1996,
linoprint on paper.

Gargaru
(MUSSELS)

You go in river, along the bank ... you go feel 'em with your hands. Boil 'em and you chuck 'em in coals and he open up.

You can have 'em with soya sauce, rice, anything.

Kathy Bird

Luis Karadada, *Slates*, 1996,
silkscreen on fabric.

DAMPER

Just get the plain flour, baking powder and mix 'em with water. Knead it
with your hand. Make a fire. Then take it out and roll it with your hands.
Roll it into a moon shape.

Wait 'til the flames die down and you just have the coals. Get a stick or a
shovel, make a shape like the damper. Then get the hot sand and chuck it
over the damper. People can make fruit damper with egg, dried fruits —
just add 'em at the end.

Linda De Lower

Jenny Drummond, *Bush Life*, 1996,
silkscreen on fabric.

Big Gums

On the trees along the river, near Fitzroy, around there. When we were schooling there we used to get 'em up the tree. You see 'em on the tree — we used to get it out with a knife and just suck on it. Sometimes they dark brown or orange.

Kathy Bird

Cecelia Riley, *Kimberley Diamonds–Bush Gums*, 1996, linoprint on paper.

Red Hill Kangaroo

Round Mount House, they stand up really high, big one, stand up like a man. You sneak 'em up with a spear and got him here ... like this ...

You eat that one, same way in a hole in the coals.

Kathy Bird

Jeanette Ishigushi, *Boomerangs*, 1996,
silkscreen on fabric.

Black Plum

Napier side ... the tree it has big purple ones, too sweet. They're like these plums you buy in Woolies.

You boil 'em and we eat 'em. When 'e boiled, put 'em outside the billycan and when 'e cooled tip 'em out.

Kathy Bird

Kathy Bird, *Ant Beds*, 1996,
linoprint on paper.

Dugong

You can marinate it in soya sauce and garlic, then cut it in thin slices and barbecue it or cook it in the coals.

Some people boil it until it's cooked, but you can steam it as well.

Lizzie Kelly

Valerie Lennard, *Sea Foods*, 1996, linoprint on paper.

GOOLIL
(FRESH WATER TURTLE)

Sometimes they cook 'em in a hole in the coals, they guts it out. You cover it with sand.

You catch 'em on the line, they find 'em by the hole in the swamp.

Valerie Lennard

Ina Kitching, *Long Neck Turtle*, 1996, silkscreen on fabric.

Catfish Curry and Rice

Cook the rice. You guts 'em out, clean 'em inside and sometime we make a stew.

When 'e boil ... when that water boil, then you mix it up with curry. Sometimes you put raw flour in the fish and mix it up.

Use catfish, barramundi, any fish, and chuck anything you think of in there; onions, cabbages, garlic, then add your curry powder.

Kathy Bird, Valerie Lennard
and Nusheba McMahon

Sonja Kurrar, *Barramundi*, 1996,
silkscreen on fabric.

EMU

You chase 'em and shoot it, or sneak 'em up.

Well, you pluck all the feathers or you can burn the feathers. First you gotta clean the guts out. Dig a hole before the fire. Put biggest mob of wood there. They put rocks in its guts, then cover it over with sheet of iron, then cook it.

It tastes like fresh meat, like chicken.

Kathy Bird
and Cecelia Riley

Waterlily Roots

You pull 'em out of the water. They are like some sort of potato under the roots. Just stick on the coals.

Annette Riley

JUDIMBAH — CHERRABUN
(FRESH WATER PRAWNS)

You can boil these up, then fry 'em with peas and other vegetables and eat
it with rice.

Annette Riley

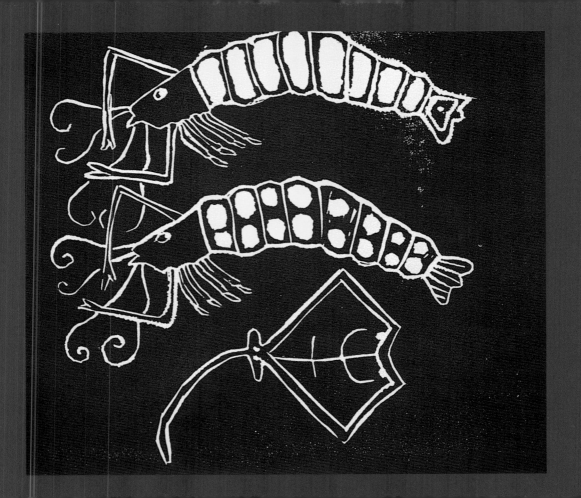

ACKNOWLEDGEMENTS

Thank you to everyone from Ngunga Designs who contributed to this book — Kay Wilson, Jeanette Ishigushi, April Wilson, Valerie Lennard, Cecelia Riley, Kathy Bird, Agnes Bird, Linda De Lower, Annette Riley, Antoinette Hunter, Pat Latham, Pamela Marshall, Nicky Dawson, Halimah Bin Karim, Nusheba McMahon, Josie Drummond, Jenny Drummond, Lizzie Kelly, Ina Kitching, Sonja Kurrar, Brenda Titum, Verna Ishigushi, Iris Edgar, Luis Karadada and Rod Lawson.

Thanks also to the following people who offered their support: Ngunga Women's Group, Derby, Jenny Wright, Artists Foundation of Western Australia, Marianne Yambo and Ernest Edney, Bruce Armstrong, Chris Armstrong, Susan Gunter, Sandra Bowkett and Lockyer, Keryn Boyer, Ruth Johnstone, Merryn Ricketson, Women's Art Registrar, Di Waite and Gwenda Flintoff, Print Council of Australia, Gerry Ryan, Silkcut Lino, Mary Anne Jebb, Robyn Tredwell, Derby/West Kimberly College of TAFE, Mark Noval and his etching press, Emily Knight, Halls Creek Language Centre, Shirley Frizelle, Healthway WA, Robyn Bowcock, Gwen and Burt Palethorpe.